Green

Shared w/ Bwdy / Lorenzo / A

The class drew th Old Hermit

To my wife Alice Edebiri,
my source and inspiration
for this rich African lore,
without whose love
and support this
book would not
have been
possible

Illustrated by Alphonso Lassiter and designed by Rose Caporaletti

Copyright © 1999 by The United African
Educational and Scholarship Foundation

ISBN 1-893811-00-X

Printed in Hong Kong

There is a rich tradition in every African country of stories and fables used in the education of young children. The fables highlight moral and ethical aspects of human behavior and relationships in an easily understandable form. In Africa, it is quite common to see a group of children gathered around an old sage listening appreciatively to old stories or fables. Typically, these fables have been handed down from generation to generation in the oral tradition of ancient African cultures. From Aesop's famous animal fables to Anansi the Spider, the consummate trickster of the Akan folktales, African fables have been a valuable source of inspiration to virtually every culture on earth.

The Old Hermit and the Boy Who Couldn't Stop Laughing is written in the spirit of this great African tradition. Although the fable's basic theme originated among the Edo-speaking people of Nigeria, it is a theme that is universal in terms of its rich moral meaning. Edo is spoken among the Bini, a proud, creative people who inhabit a very old city in Nigeria's midwestern region called "Benin." Benin City is the governmental center of a legendary monarchy dating back to biblical days. Commonly referred to as the "Ancient Kingdom of Benin" by world historians, this ancient African city is renowned for having produced one of the world's most glorious artistic legacies in its awe-inspiring bronze castings and elegant wood and ivory carvings and sculptures.

Nigeria boasts a population of more than one hundred million people made up of 250 different linguistic or ethnic groups. The largest and most widely known of these groups are the Yoruba, the Hausa, and the Ibo. The country covers an expanse of 356,669 square miles of lush green forests, rivers, agricultural plateaus and rich mineral deposits. The tale of an old recluse and a taunting little boy arises out of this fascinating geography and these cultures. As are all fables, this story is both allegory and myth. But the idea of children teasing or making fun of the aged and the deformed is all too real and familiar. The story, thus, is one likely to find moral resonance for all who read it.

There was once an old hermit who lived at the top of a <u>densely</u> forested mountain that overlooked a <u>bustling</u> West African city. The old hermit seldom went down to the city, because each time he did people stared and <u>gawked</u> at him, which made him feel uncomfortable and sad. The old hermit was not of ordinary appearance. He was <u>odd</u> looking. He never shaved. He wore the same old dirty and ragged clothes every day. And his legs were bent and crooked, so that he walked with an almost comic shuffle. But perhaps the most striking feature of the old hermit was his head. It was <u>enormous</u>.

One day, the old hermit ran out of his favorite pipe tobacco and decided to go down to the city to purchase a new supply. As he hopped and shuffled his way along the busy city streets, he met little nine-year-old Osade (O-sá-day) on the way. Osade was a playful village boy who sometimes delighted in mocking or making fun of the elderly and the physically deformed. Osade was accompanied by a young couple whom he met on the road as they were returning from the town market. The young couple and Osade lived next-door to each other in a nearby village.

As they were passing the old hermit on the street, the young couple urged Osade not to stare at him, but to turn his face the other way until they passed. They strongly cautioned him, saying "Above all else, Osade, do not laugh at that strange old man!" But Osade, seeing the old hermit shuffling along with his hopping walk and <u>oversized</u> head, thought him the funniest sight he had ever seen. Unable to contain himself, Osade burst into a loud, hardy laugh—"Ha, ha, ha, ha, ha, ha!"

At first, the old hermit pretended that he did not hear Osade laughing at him. He even tried to speed up his shuffle to avoid the teasing. But Osade ran after the hermit, pointing and <u>waggling</u> his finger at him, and even rolling over on the ground, holding his belly and shaking with <u>outrageous</u> laughter—"Ha, ha, ha, ha, ha, ha!"

The young couple tried to stop Osade from laughing and tried frantically to whisk him away. But Osade would have none of that. He was having too much fun.

Osade was so enraptured with his prank that he began to dance and skip around the fleeing old hermit, teasing and taunting him as the hermit hopped and shuffled along. The hermit tried his best to get away, but he could not. Osade was just too quick for him.

Then suddenly, and without warning, the old hermit stopped abruptly. He turned around quickly and snapped his fingers at Osade and said, "Little boy, as you are now laughing, so shall you continue laughing for the rest of your life!" Osade, who was still laughing, was finally restrained by the young couple, who wrestled him to the ground and sat on top of him, allowing the old hermit to go on his way.

Some thirty minutes later, Osade and the young couple had reached their village. The couple ran straight to Osade's parents and reported what had happened. Upon hearing their account, and seeing that their son was still laughing, the parents became extremely worried. They hoped desperately that the old hermit had not placed a spell on their son. Not being sure of it, the parents ran quickly to the village chief and frantically told their story. After hearing of the encounter, the chief sent them immediately to consult with the village griot (grē-o), a kindly old storyteller who also possessed mysterious powers.

Meanwhile, Osade was still laughing. He made constant snickering sounds that were periodically interrupted by outbursts of loud, hearty laughter.

ater at the home of the griot, Osade's parents waited to hear their son's fate. Finally, the griot emerged from his hut carrying an old leather pouch containing small cowrie shells, pebbles, old, dried pieces of palm kernel, and other strange looking objects that gave him the ability to see into the future as well as other mysterious powers.

The griot sat down on the ground in front of his hut and motioned for Osade's parents to sit with him. He then emptied his leather pouch into his hand and scattered the objects on the ground in front of them. After a few minutes of careful examination of the objects, the griot told Osade's parents that the hermit had indeed placed a spell on their son, because he had persistently laughed at and made fun of the old hermit. The griot told the parents that the hermit's spell was not an ordinary one, but a special kind of spell that probably could not be lifted by anyone. Upon hearing this, Osade's parents were completely overcome by grief.

Seeing their great agony, the griot told the parents to take courage, because there was an outside chance that the parents themselves could do something to break the spell. But he quickly cautioned them that what he had in mind might not work. He told the parents to have their son taken through a series of ancient ancestral ceremonies, which required amulets and precious stones that would be very costly to obtain. He told them to observe strictly all of the rules and injunctions of the ceremonies and then to hope for the best. The griot admitted to the parents that he could not guarantee success, because the source from which the old hermit drew his powers was greater than any magic or sorcery he himself had ever known.

So Osade's parents, following the griot's instructions, set out immediately to see their son through the various ceremonies and rituals required to lift the spell.

A whole month had passed, and Osade was still laughing. Osade's parents had done all they could do. They had spent all their money and all they could beg or borrow to have the ceremonies performed, but with no results. Osade's parents were overcome by a great sadness.

Then one day, as if by a miracle, Osade abruptly stopped laughing. The entire village came out to see. No one could believe it, or dared try to explain it. For weeks Osade had been laughing continually, but now he had stopped. He was normal again, except for his head. It had become extremely large, like that of the hermit. But Osade didn't seem to mind, nor did his parents. Osade's parents were so happy that he had finally stopped laughing that his sudden physical disfigurement did not seem to matter. It was a small price to pay, they believed, compared to their child having to go through life laughing every minute of his days.

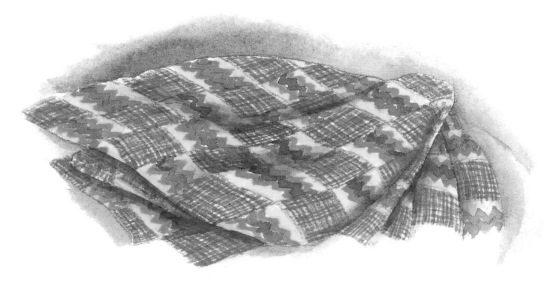

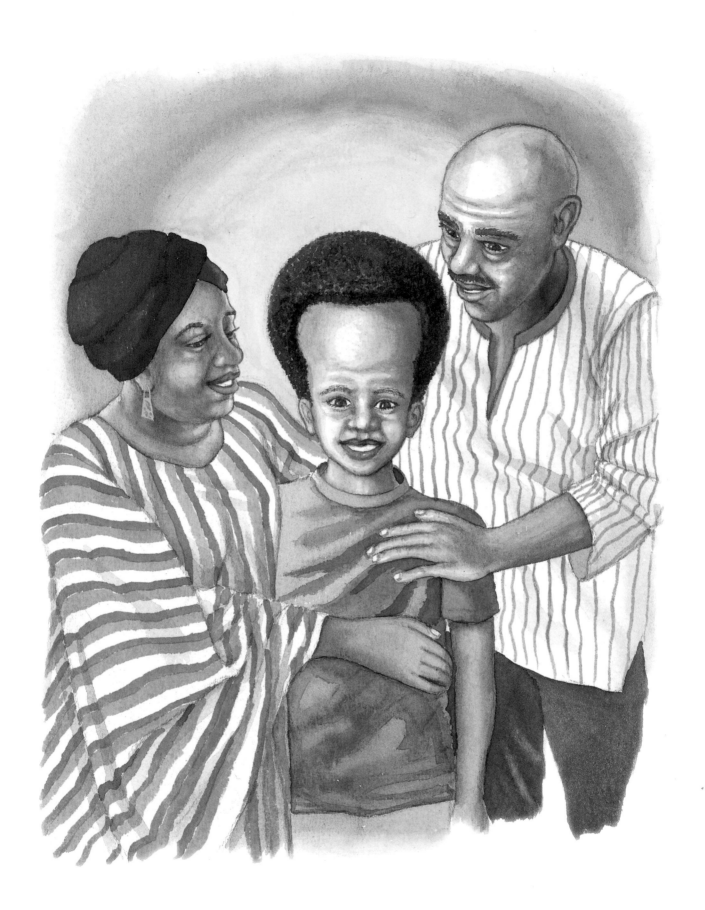

No one except the village griot knew what
or who had broken the spell of the old hermit.
Everyone else was totally mystified. Everyone
knew that the spell was one that could not be broken.
But the griot had read the signs early and knew that the
only person capable of lifting that kind of spell was the
very person who had cast it in the first place, no one else.
So the griot, realizing that Osade's fate was in the hands
of the hermit, had secretly gone to him and had begged
him to release Osade from the spell. The griot assured
the hermit that the boy and his parents had suffered
enough, and that he was certain
that the incident would
serve as a warning to
other children not to
mock or make fun
of the aged or the
physically deformed.

The incident had a powerful impact on Osade and his parents. The boy had undergone a complete change in attitude. Although he was sometimes the object of curious stares due to his suddenly overgrown head, he had become exceedingly polite and respectful to everyone, particularly to the elderly and the disfigured.

Several years passed, and Osade the boy grew to young adulthood. One day, as he was walking down the main street of the city, he came upon the same old hermit, shuffling along with his hopping walk and oversized head just as before. This time Osade did not laugh. He had learned a very dear lesson and paid a very dear price. He was a man now.

Emota, Benin "tree of life"

K. Christopher Toussaint has focused his attention on Africa and the African-American experience since early adolescence. Born and raised in Orangeburg, South Carolina, during Jim Crow, he attended Wilkerson Senior High, then the town's only black senior high school. Seizing an opportunity to travel up north, he left high school and became a migrant farm worker. After three drudging years of harvesting crops in New York, Pennsylvania, and Florida, he found his way to New York City, where he lived with his older sister and her family. Having finally graduated from high school, he studied at City College of New York and Hunter College. He then traveled to Nigeria, West Africa, returning several years later with a Nigerian wife (Alice Edebiri). Upon their return, he went back to school, enrolling first at the University of Pennsylvania, where he earned a B.B.A. at the Wharton School of Business, and then at Temple University, where he earned both an M.A. and a Ph.D. in sociology.

Teaching sociology and race relations courses at a number of colleges and universities, including the University of Pennsylvania, Dr. Toussaint became more and more convinced that the time had come for blacks to take their educational destiny into their own hands. Thus, in 1997, he and his wife founded the United African Educational and Scholarship Foundation (UAESF), a nonprofit, charitable organization that attempts to address the myriad educational problems that persistently confront black students on all educational levels in the United States and abroad. In addressing these problems, UAESF seeks to provide educational support to black students in a variety of innovative ways, including providing scholarships to black children at the primary and middle-school levels and mentoring and tutoring black students, one-on-one, particularly at-risk urban black high school students. *The Old Hermit and the Boy Who Couldn't Stop Laughing* is only the first in a series of African fables that UAESF will publish. These fables will provide shared reading and conversational experiences for parents and children, along with some geography, history, and cultural lore of Africa. The self-funding of the foundation's goals, using the fables as a principal means, is an embodiment of the idea of self-determination for black institutions—a long-held idea that must be fully realized to create a better future for us all.

Future book publications in our African Fables for Children Series:

The Parrot, the Schoolmaster, and the Village Thieves

The Servant and the Rich Merchant

How the Chimp Became Sole Owner of the Bananna Tree

The Blind Begger and the Innkeeper

The Little Bird and the King

The Lion, the Hare, and the Hunter

The Peacock and the Turkey

The Monkey and the Giraffe

The Springbok and the Cheetah

The Lark and the Nightingale

The Skunk and the Bramble

The Rhinoceros and the Egret

The Aardvark and the Ant

The Swan and the Geese